A JOURNEY THROUGH LENT

Reflecting on
Christ's Sacrifice for Us

A JOURNEY THROUGH LENT

Reflecting on Christ's Sacrifice for Us

A Seven-Session Study Guide by
Redeemer Presbyterian Church

gospel in life

A Journey through Lent: Reflecting on Christ's Sacrifice for Us
A Seven-Session Study Guide from Redeemer Presbyterian Church

Copyright © 2016 by Redeemer Presbyterian Church, located at
1166 Avenue of the Americas, 16th floor, New York, NY 10036.

ISBN-13: 978-1-944549-04-6

A Journey through Lent: Reflecting on Christ's Sacrifice for Us was written and
developed by the staff of Redeemer Presbyterian Church of New York City.

Cover and interior design: Lee Marcum

Printed in the United States of America

CONTENTS

Introduction   5

Study #1   Prayer of Confession   7
Psalm 32

Study #2   Prayer of Seeking   15
Psalm 34

Study #3   Prayer of Thirst   23
Psalms 42-43

Study #4   Prayer of Rest   31
Psalm 91

Study #5   Prayer for the World   37
Psalm 98

Study #6   Prayer for the King   43
Psalm 110

Study #7   Prayer for Security   49
Psalm 16

Leader's Notes   57

INTRODUCTION

For the season of Lent, Dr. Timothy Keller and the pastors at Redeemer Presbyterian Church preached a series of sermons on the psalms. This series, "Psalms for the Journey," served as instruction for congregants spending a season of reflection and repentance in preparation for Easter Sunday. The seven-week study guide was developed by church staff to accompany the weekly sermons.

What is Lent? The word "Lent" comes from the Old English word "lengten," which simply means "spring"—when the days lengthen and new life springs forth. It is a time in which we anticipate the victory of the light and life of Christ over the darkness of sin and death. It is, to borrow a phrase from C.S. Lewis, a season of a kind of "happiness and wonder that makes you serious."

Just as we carefully prepare for big events in our personal lives, such as a wedding or commencement, Lent invites us to make our hearts ready for remembering Jesus' death and resurrection. It is our prayer that as you ready your heart over the next 40 days of Lent, these studies will be fresh reminders of the truth we need to continually speak to our souls. These psalms address the reality of our broken humanity and recognize the world is not as it should be. But even as the days lengthen and grow brighter, these prayers point to the end of the story—Easter Sunday and the ultimate restoration of all things.

Each study will take you through four main ideas:

1. *The Text*. What are the main points of the Scripture passage?

2. *The Text in the Bigger Story*. How does this text connect to the larger narrative of the Bible?

3. *Jesus Completing the Story*. How does this text culminate in the life and work of Jesus?

4. *Living Out the Story*. How does this text move us, in practical ways, toward greater faith and repentance?

Keep these in mind as you go through each passage and process them as a group. There are additional notes to guide discussion leaders at the back of this book.

Finally, as your group studies the Bible together, it is helpful to remember that since all Scripture is revelation about God and Jesus Christ is the culmination of this, then fundamentally all Scripture (both Old Testament and New Testament) is about him—his life, death and resurrection (Luke 24:27, 45-47).

Prayer of Confession

SCRIPTURE

Psalm 32 (NIV)

[1] Blessed is the one
  whose transgressions are forgiven,
  whose sins are covered.
[2] Blessed is the one
  whose sin the LORD does not count against them
  and in whose spirit is no deceit.

[3] When I kept silent,
  my bones wasted away
  through my groaning all day long.
[4] For day and night
  your hand was heavy on me;
my strength was sapped
  as in the heat of summer.

[5] Then I acknowledged my sin to you
  and did not cover up my iniquity.
I said, "I will confess
  my transgressions to the LORD."
And you forgave
  the guilt of my sin.

[6] Therefore let all the faithful pray to you
  while you may be found;
surely the rising of the mighty waters
  will not reach them.

[7] You are my hiding place;
    you will protect me from trouble
    and surround me with songs of deliverance.

[8] I will instruct you and teach you in the way you should go;
    I will counsel you with my loving eye on you.
[9] Do not be like the horse or the mule,
    which have no understanding
but must be controlled by bit and bridle
    or they will not come to you.
[10] Many are the woes of the wicked,
    but the LORD's unfailing love
    surrounds the one who trusts in him.

[11] Rejoice in the LORD and be glad, you righteous;
    sing, all you who are upright in heart!

DISCUSSION

Goal of This Study: To understand that renewal happens only as we understand the dangers of sin, the nature of joyful repentance, and God's gift of forgiveness.

Background Information: As we enter the season of Lent, a helpful starting point is to consider what Lent means, both literally and figuratively. The word "Lent" comes from the Old English word "lengten," which simply means "spring"—when the days lengthen and new life springs forth. It is a time in which we anticipate the victory of the light and life of Christ over the darkness of sin and death. It is, to borrow a phrase from C.S. Lewis, a season of a kind of "happiness and wonder that makes you serious."

Lent is traditionally observed in the church calendar during the 40 days prior to Easter. It is a season of joyful repentance. It is joyful, because the goal of repentance is to bring renewal to our lives. It is a time of remembering that we are weak, unable to change ourselves, and dependent on God for transformation. The season culminates with the week of Christ's passion and death on the cross, where we see that nothing less than Jesus' sacrificial death is required to heal us and make us new.

These truths penetrate our hearts primarily through prayer. Therefore, throughout Lent we will look at prayers from the psalms in which these truths are highlighted. We begin this week with Psalm 32, which addresses the seriousness of sin and God's willingness to forgive us.

The Text

1. Overall, the psalm rejoices in forgiveness and the joy it brings. But first, what do verses 3 and 4 tell us about sin and its consequences? Does this ring true to your experience?

2. What obstacles do we face in believing that sin brings harm to us? Where have you personally encountered difficulty believing that sin is destructive?

3. What is involved in genuine repentance, according to verse 5?

4. Remorse or fear may lead to change because we want to avoid the consequences of a wrong behavior. Why is true repentance done out of love for God and a desire to avoid grieving him more appropriate and effective?

The Text in the Bigger Story

Read Romans 4:4-12 with Psalm 32 in mind.

[4] Now to the one who works, wages are not credited as a gift but as an obligation. [5] However, to the one who does not work but trusts God who justifies the ungodly, their faith is credited as righteousness. [6] David says the same thing when he speaks of the blessedness of the one to whom God credits righteousness apart from works:

> [7] "Blessed are those
>> whose transgressions are forgiven,
>> whose sins are covered.
> [8] Blessed is the one
>> whose sin the Lord will never count against them."

[9] Is this blessedness only for the circumcised, or also for the uncircumcised? We have been saying that Abraham's faith was credited to him as righteousness. [10] Under what circumstances was it credited? Was it after he was circumcised, or before? It was not after, but before! [11] And he received circumcision as a sign, a seal of the

righteousness that he had by faith while he was still uncircumcised. So then, he is the father of all who believe but have not been circumcised, in order that righteousness might be credited to them. [12] And he is then also the father of the circumcised who not only are circumcised but who also follow in the footsteps of the faith that our father Abraham had before he was circumcised.

5. **What does the language of Psalm 32 (and quoted in Romans 4) teach us about what is involved in the wonderful gift of forgiveness?**

Jesus Completing the Story

6. **How does the sacrificial death of Jesus enrich our understanding of God's forgiveness and lead us to a place of genuine heartfelt and joyful repentance?**

Living Out the Story

7. In what ways do we fail to own our sin and what effect does that have on us?

8. Take a moment to consider a recurring sin in your life. What is at the root of that sin? How can you begin to cut off that sin at the root?

PRAYER

Throughout Lent we will practice meditation on the psalm we are studying, using the following steps:

○ One group member reads Psalm 32 out loud.

○ Allow 5 minutes for silent reflection on the psalm, considering a word, phrase or verse that captured your mind or attention. Prayerfully reflect on it before God and meditate on the obstacles that prevent you from fully believing or obeying God.

○ Re-read the psalm out loud once more, with two or more group members facilitating the oral reading.

○ Go around the group, with each person sharing the one phrase that captured their thinking, with no additional commentary provided, simply the biblical text that was meaningful to them.

Close in prayer, giving thanks for the things God has taught you during the study of the psalm.

Prayer of Seeking

SCRIPTURE

Psalm 34 (NIV)

[1] I will extol the LORD at all times;
　his praise will always be on my lips.
[2] I will glory in the LORD;
　let the afflicted hear and rejoice.
[3] Glorify the LORD with me;
　let us exalt his name together.

[4] I sought the LORD, and he answered me;
　he delivered me from all my fears.
[5] Those who look to him are radiant;
　their faces are never covered with shame.
[6] This poor man called, and the LORD heard him;
　he saved him out of all his troubles.
[7] The angel of the LORD encamps around those who fear him,
　and he delivers them.

[8] Taste and see that the LORD is good;
　blessed is the one who takes refuge in him.
[9] Fear the LORD, you his holy people,
　for those who fear him lack nothing.
[10] The lions may grow weak and hungry,
　but those who seek the LORD lack no good thing.
[11] Come, my children, listen to me;
　I will teach you the fear of the LORD.
[12] Whoever of you loves life
　and desires to see many good days,

¹³ keep your tongue from evil
   and your lips from telling lies.
¹⁴ Turn from evil and do good;
   seek peace and pursue it.

¹⁵ The eyes of the LORD are on the righteous,
   and his ears are attentive to their cry;
¹⁶ but the face of the LORD is against those who do evil,
   to blot out their name from the earth.

¹⁷ The righteous cry out, and the LORD hears them;
   he delivers them from all their troubles.
¹⁸ The LORD is close to the brokenhearted
   and saves those who are crushed in spirit.

¹⁹ The righteous person may have many troubles,
   but the LORD delivers him from them all;
²⁰ he protects all his bones,
   not one of them will be broken.

²¹ Evil will slay the wicked;
   the foes of the righteous will be condemned.
²² The LORD will rescue his servants;
   no one who takes refuge in him will be condemned.

DISCUSSION

Goal of This Study: Though suffering is inevitable and most often out of our control, our response to suffering is dependent on our choices. The goal of the study is to learn how in times of suffering to fear the Lord, rather than our circumstances. This posture, admonished throughout Scripture, places us under God's protection and allows us to experience his glory.

Background Information: The 40 days of Lent correspond to Jesus' 40 days of testing in the wilderness at the beginning of his ministry. Just as Jesus used Scripture during his days of testing, so too, we turn to the psalms to help us in times of difficulty. The psalms help us in times of self-examination and dryness, leading us to see our need for grace and to teach us to long again for Christ's redemption and resurrection.

Though impossible to see in English, Psalm 34 is an acrostic psalm, meaning every verse begins with the next letter of the Hebrew alphabet. So the psalm could be called the "ABCs for a Crisis."[1] It comprehensively covers what to do when afflicted (v. 2), filled with fears (v. 4), surrounded by troubles (vv. 6, 17), brokenhearted, crushed in spirit (v. 18) and in many afflictions (v. 19). In short, this psalm addresses what to do when bad things happen. If we heed David's advice, we will seek the Lord and find him to be our refuge during times of suffering.

The Text

1. **Having experienced great suffering, David now urges the afflicted to do what he did: cry out to God and experience his protection and peace (verses 1-3). Have you experienced suffering? If so, where did you turn?**

---

[1] Gordon J. Wenham and Alec J. Motyer, "Psalms" in *New Bible Commentary: 21 Century Edition* (Westmont, Ill: IVP Academic), 506.

2. David attests that when we seek God in these times, we can experience deliverance and liberation from the power of suffering in our lives (verses 4-7). As a group, consider aloud what deliverance, liberation and even protection from suffering might look like?

3. God promises through David that when you take refuge in him you will lack "no good thing." Many of us know this in our head, yet in our daily lives we seek less reliable sources for satisfaction or security. Why is it so hard to believe that in God we will lack nothing we really need? How might David's language here move us to greater degrees of trust and pleasure in God?

The Text in the Bigger Story

Read together Romans 8:1,18-37.

[1] Therefore, there is now no condemnation for those who are in Christ Jesus

[18] I consider that our present sufferings are not worth comparing with the glory that will be revealed in us. [19] For the creation waits in eager expectation for the children of God to be revealed. [20] For the creation was subjected to frustration, not by its own choice, but by the will of the one who subjected it, in hope [21] that the creation itself will be liberated from its bondage to decay and brought into the freedom and glory of the children of God.

[22] We know that the whole creation has been groaning as in the pains of childbirth right up to the present time. [23] Not only so, but we ourselves, who have the firstfruits of the Spirit, groan inwardly as we wait eagerly for our adoption to sonship, the redemption of our bodies. [24] For in this hope we were saved. But hope that is seen is no hope at all. Who hopes for what they already have? [25] But if we hope for what we do not yet have, we wait for it patiently.

[26] In the same way, the Spirit helps us in our weakness. We do not know what we ought to pray for, but the Spirit himself intercedes for us through wordless groans. [27] And he who searches our hearts knows the mind of the Spirit, because the Spirit intercedes for God's people in accordance with the will of God.

[28] And we know that in all things God works for the good of those who love him, who have been called according to his purpose. [29] For those God foreknew he also predestined to be conformed to the image of his Son, that he might be the firstborn among many brothers and sisters. [30] And those he predestined, he also called; those he called, he also justified; those he justified, he also glorified.

[31] What, then, shall we say in response to these things? If God is for us, who can be against us? [32] He who did not spare his own Son, but gave him up for us all—how will he not also, along with him, graciously give us all things? [33] Who will bring any charge against those whom God has chosen? It is God who justifies. [34] Who then is the one who condemns? No one. Christ Jesus who died—more than that, who was raised to life—is at the right hand of God and is also interceding for us. [35] Who shall separate us from the love of Christ? Shall trouble or hardship or persecution or famine or nakedness or danger or sword? [36] As it is written:

> "For your sake we face death all day long;
> we are considered as sheep to be slaughtered."

[37] No, in all these things we are more than conquerors through him who loved us.

4. From Genesis to Revelation, the Bible reveals God's plan to bring creation from suffering into glory. According to Romans 8, what can we learn about our own suffering?

Jesus Completing the Story

5. What do we learn about our suffering and our ability to trust God in light of Jesus' death on the cross?

Living Out the Story

6. How does Christianity uniquely redeem our suffering?

PRAYER

Throughout Lent we will practice meditation on the psalm we are studying, using the following steps:

○ One group member reads Psalm 34 out loud.

○ Allow 5 minutes for silent reflection on the psalm, considering a word, phrase or verse that captured your mind or attention. Prayerfully reflect on it before God and meditate on the obstacles that prevent you from fully believing or obeying God.

○ Re-read the psalm out loud once more, with two or more group members facilitating the oral reading.

○ Go around the group, with each person sharing the one phrase that captured their thinking, with no additional commentary provided, simply the biblical text that was meaningful to them.

Close in prayer, giving thanks for the things God has taught you during the study of the psalm.

Prayer of Thirst

SCRIPTURE

Psalms 42-43 (NIV)

[1] As the deer pants for streams of water,
   so my soul pants for you, my God.
[2] My soul thirsts for God, for the living God.
   When can I go and meet with God?
[3] My tears have been my food
   day and night,
while people say to me all day long,
   "Where is your God?"
[4] These things I remember
   as I pour out my soul:
how I used to go to the house of God
   under the protection of the Mighty One
with shouts of joy and praise
   among the festive throng.

[5] Why, my soul, are you downcast?
   Why so disturbed within me?
Put your hope in God,
   for I will yet praise him,
   my Savior and my God.

[6] My soul is downcast within me;
   therefore I will remember you
from the land of the Jordan,
   the heights of Hermon—from Mount Mizar.
[7] Deep calls to deep

in the roar of your waterfalls;
all your waves and breakers
    have swept over me.

[8] By day the LORD directs his love,
    at night his song is with me—
    a prayer to the God of my life.

[9] I say to God my Rock,
    "Why have you forgotten me?
Why must I go about mourning,
    oppressed by the enemy?"
[10] My bones suffer mortal agony
    as my foes taunt me,
saying to me all day long,
    "Where is your God?"

[11] Why, my soul, are you downcast?
    Why so disturbed within me?
Put your hope in God,
    for I will yet praise him,
    my Savior and my God.

Psalm 43

[1] Vindicate me, my God,
    and plead my cause
    against an unfaithful nation.
Rescue me from those who are
    deceitful and wicked.
[2] You are God my stronghold.
    Why have you rejected me?
Why must I go about mourning,
    oppressed by the enemy?
[3] Send me your light and your faithful care,
    let them lead me;
let them bring me to your holy mountain,
    to the place where you dwell.
[4] Then I will go to the altar of God,
    to God, my joy and my delight.

I will praise you with the lyre,
  O God, my God.

[5] Why, my soul, are you downcast?
  Why so disturbed within me?
Put your hope in God,
  for I will yet praise him,
  my Savior and my God.

DISCUSSION

Goal of This Study: To experience how Christ changes our hopes when we are honest with ourselves and with God during times of spiritual dryness.

Background Information: We are entering the third week of Lent, a season of joyful repentance. Remember that repentance is joyful, because it allows our relationship with God to resume its intimacy. It is a time of reckoning that we are weak, unable to change ourselves, and dependent on God for transformation.

The season culminates with the week of Christ's passion and death on the cross, where we see that nothing less than Jesus' sacrificial death is required to heal us and make us new. These truths penetrate our hearts primarily through prayer. Therefore, throughout Lent we are studying prayers from the psalms in which these truths are highlighted.

This week, we will focus on Psalms 42 and 43, which are a lament. Most scholars consider Psalms 42 and 43 to be two parts of a single poem that has one refrain, "Why so downcast, O my soul" echoing throughout it. The writer, one of the "sons of Korah," mourns his absence from corporate worship, and it becomes to him a cause of grief that is aggravated by the taunts of enemies. The psalm moves from near despair to surging confidence, from desperate spiritual thirst to rejoicing in God.

Our modern experience of spiritually dry times may be circumstantially different than that of the psalmist, yet we can find commonality in the feelings and actions that we share with the writer and in the satisfaction he finds in God, who is the ultimate source of hope.

The Text

1. **Describe what the psalmist is experiencing and feeling, focusing primarily on Psalm 42:1-5. When do you tend to think or feel this way?**

2. **In this passage, what do you see that might have triggered his hopelessness? What don't you see? Discuss in your group other factors for spiritual apathy that are not in this psalm.**

3. **One of the breakthroughs in prayer is to learn how to lament honestly and rightly. What did the psalmist do to remedy his downcast heart?**

The Text in the Bigger Story

Read together Mark 15:24-39.

24 And they crucified him. Dividing up his clothes, they cast lots to see what each would get.

25 It was nine in the morning when they crucified him. 26 The written notice of the charge against him read: the king of the jews.

27 They crucified two rebels with him, one on his right and one on his left. [28] 29 Those who passed by hurled insults at him, shaking their heads and saying, "So! You who are going to destroy the temple and build it in three days, 30 come down from the cross and save yourself!" 31 In the same way the chief priests and the teachers of the law mocked him among themselves. "He saved others," they said, "but he can't save himself! 32 Let this Messiah, this king of Israel, come down now from the cross, that we may see and believe." Those crucified with him also heaped insults on him.

33 At noon, darkness came over the whole land until three in the afternoon. 34 And at three in the afternoon Jesus cried out in a loud voice, "Eloi, Eloi, lema sabachthani?" (which means "My God, my God, why have you forsaken me?").

35 When some of those standing near heard this, they said, "Listen, he's calling Elijah."

36 Someone ran, filled a sponge with wine vinegar, put it on a staff, and offered it to Jesus to drink. "Now leave him alone. Let's see if Elijah comes to take him down," he said.

37 With a loud cry, Jesus breathed his last.

38 The curtain of the temple was torn in two from top to bottom. 39 And when the centurion, who stood there in front of Jesus, saw how he died, he said, "Surely this man was the Son of God!"

4. Compare and contrast the mocking of the psalmist and the mocking of Christ on the cross. Why is the psalmist being mocked? Why is Jesus being mocked?

Being mocked by self

Jesus Completing the Story

5. How can Jesus' thirsting and experience of being forsaken for you change you, so that you seek hope and satisfaction in him?

Living Out the Story

6. What would it look like for you to hope in God in the midst of a current disturbing time? How can your community help each other?

PRAYER

Throughout Lent we will practice meditation on the psalms we are studying, using the following steps:

○ One or more group members read aloud Psalms 42-43.

○ Allow 5 minutes for silent reflection on the psalm, considering a word, phrase or verse that captured your mind or attention. Prayerfully reflect on it before God and meditate on the obstacles that prevent you from fully believing or obeying God.

○ Re-read the psalm out loud once more, with two or more group members facilitating the oral reading.

○ Go around the group, with each person sharing the one phrase that captured their thinking, with no additional commentary provided, simply the biblical text that was meaningful to them.

Close in prayer, giving thanks for the things God has taught you during the study of these psalms.

Prayer of Rest

SCRIPTURE

Psalm 91 (NIV)

¹ Whoever dwells in the shelter of the Most High
  will rest in the shadow of the Almighty.
² I will say of the LORD, "He is my refuge and my fortress,
  my God, in whom I trust."

³ Surely he will save you
  from the fowler's snare
  and from the deadly pestilence.
⁴ He will cover you with his feathers,
  and under his wings you will find refuge;
  his faithfulness will be your shield and rampart.
⁵ You will not fear the terror of night,
  nor the arrow that flies by day,
⁶ nor the pestilence that stalks in the darkness,
  nor the plague that destroys at midday.
⁷ A thousand may fall at your side,
  ten thousand at your right hand,
  but it will not come near you.
⁸ You will only observe with your eyes
  and see the punishment of the wicked.

⁹ If you say, "The LORD is my refuge,"
  and you make the Most High your dwelling,
¹⁰ no harm will overtake you,
  no disaster will come near your tent.
¹¹ For he will command his angels concerning you

to guard you in all your ways;
¹² they will lift you up in their hands,
   so that you will not strike your foot against a stone.
¹³ You will tread on the lion and the cobra;
   you will trample the great lion and the serpent.

¹⁴ "Because he loves me," says the LORD, "I will rescue him;
   I will protect him, for he acknowledges my name.
¹⁵ He will call on me, and I will answer him;
   I will be with him in trouble,
   I will deliver him and honor him.
¹⁶ With long life I will satisfy him
   and show him my salvation."

DISCUSSION

Goal of This Study: The goal of this study is to realize that Jesus, because he is completely good and trustworthy, gives rest from the stresses and troubles of life to those who trust him.

Background Information: We are entering the fourth week of Lent, a season of joyful repentance. Remember that repentance is joyful because the goal is to bring renewal to our lives. Lent corresponds to Jesus' time in the wilderness, where he hungered and thirsted for 40 days. We are studying specific psalms that help us in times of self-examination, difficulty, and dryness, and they will lead us to see our need of grace and teach us to long again for Jesus' redemption and resurrection. The season culminates with the week of Jesus' journey to the cross where we see that nothing less than his sacrificial death is required to heal us and make us new. The psalms teach us to pray so that these truths will penetrate our hearts.

Psalm 91 is our focus this week. This personal psalm describes the peace and rest that Christians can have during all moments of stress, dangers and challenges. The entire psalm highlights the fact that we are always secure because God is totally trustworthy. The astounding truths explored through the lens of the psalmist's experience make it a life-giving personal prayer that equips Christians for everyday challenges.

The Text

1. Throughout the psalm the writer assumes that people need rest from the stresses and troubles of life. How do you identify with that need?

2. The first four verses of Psalm 91 establish the foundational principle that God protects his loved ones. Consider the descriptions that the psalmist uses in verses 1 to 4, and envision together what protection from God is like. How is God a defense and rest to those who trust him?

3. The psalmist writes bold statements concerning the protection God provides for those who trust in him (verses 5-13). What do you think these statements mean? What do they *not* mean?

The Text in the Bigger Story

Read Matthew 4:1-11 about the temptation of Jesus by Satan.

[4] Then Jesus was led by the Spirit into the wilderness to be tempted by the devil. [2] After fasting forty days and forty nights, he was hungry. [3] The tempter came to him and said, "If you are the Son of God, tell these stones to become bread."

[4] Jesus answered, "It is written: 'Man shall not live on bread alone, but on every word that comes from the mouth of God.'"

[5] Then the devil took him to the holy city and had him stand on the highest point of the temple. [6] "If you are the Son of God," he said, "throw yourself down. For it is written:

> "'He will command his angels concerning you,
>   and they will lift you up in their hands,
>   so that you will not strike your foot against a stone.'"

[7] Jesus answered him, "It is also written: 'Do not put the Lord your God to the test.'"

[8] Again, the devil took him to a very high mountain and showed him all the kingdoms of the world and their splendor. [9] "All this I will give you," he said, "if you will bow down and worship me."

[10] Jesus said to him, "Away from me, Satan! For it is written: 'Worship the Lord your God, and serve him only.'"

[11] Then the devil left him, and angels came and attended him.

4. In light of the 40 days of Lent and this season of spiritual discipline, what stood out to you as you read about Jesus' 40 days in the wilderness?

5. What do you learn about the craftiness of the tempter?

Jesus Completing the Story

6. Consider together Matthew 26:36-46. What do we learn about the suffering of Jesus in Gethsemane? How do the promises of Psalm 91 apply to this suffering of Jesus?

Living Out the Story

7. God is speaking directly to us in verses 14-16 of the psalm. What does he tell us to do to experience his promises of protection? What would it look like for you to live out these practical ways of trusting God?

PRAYER

Throughout Lent we will practice meditation on the psalm we are studying, using the following steps:

- One group member reads Psalm 91 out loud.

- Allow 5 minutes for silent reflection on the psalm, considering a word, phrase or verse that captured your mind or attention. Prayerfully reflect on it before God and meditate on the obstacles that prevent you from fully believing or obeying God.

- Re-read the psalm out loud once more, with two or more group members facilitating the oral reading.

- Go around the group, with each person sharing the one phrase that captured their thinking, with no additional commentary provided, simply the biblical text that was meaningful to them.

Close in prayer, giving thanks for the things God has taught you during the study of the psalm.

STUDY #5
Prayer for the World

SCRIPTURE

Psalm 98 (NIV)

¹ Sing to the LORD a new song,
   for he has done marvelous things;
his right hand and his holy arm
   have worked salvation for him.
² The LORD has made his salvation known
   and revealed his righteousness to the nations.
³ He has remembered his love
   and his faithfulness to Israel;
all the ends of the earth have seen
   the salvation of our God.

⁴ Shout for joy to the LORD, all the earth,
   burst into jubilant song with music;
⁵ make music to the LORD with the harp,
   with the harp and the sound of singing,
⁶ with trumpets and the blast of the ram's horn—
   shout for joy before the LORD, the King.

⁷ Let the sea resound, and everything in it,
   the world, and all who live in it.
⁸ Let the rivers clap their hands,
   let the mountains sing together for joy;
⁹ let them sing before the LORD,
   for he comes to judge the earth.
He will judge the world in righteousness
   and the peoples with equity.

DISCUSSION

Goal of This Study: The goal of this study is to understand that Christ's salvation brings a new song of joy to all the world.

Background Information: We are entering the fifth week of Lent, a season of joyful repentance. Remember that repentance is joyful because the goal is to bring renewal to our lives through removing the barrier to intimacy with God. As Lent corresponds to Jesus' 40 days of testing in the wilderness, we have been studying specific psalms that help us in times of self-examination, difficulty, and spiritual dryness.

As we get closer to Easter, when Jesus will turn history upside down by demonstrating through his suffering, death, and resurrection that he is the King above all kings, we turn our thoughts to praise. Psalm 98 is the object of our focus this week. This psalm reads like a loud exclamation of praise for God's great salvation to all the world. Joy and praise lead naturally to sharing with others so that ultimately the world will know of God's righteousness and goodness. The joy found in the finished work of salvation through Jesus is not just for Christians, but for the entire world. From first to last, Psalm 98 is a hymn that teaches us to praise God.

The Text

1. **Commentators call Psalm 98 a victory psalm. What kind of victory would the original readers have been thinking about when they read this psalm? How does this compare to the victory we can experience today?**

2. In verse 1, the psalmist says, "Sing to the Lord a new song." Then in verses 4 through 6 he describes the praise. How does seeing the marvelous works of God prompt us to praise? What does praise do in our lives?

3. How do God's saving acts "reveal his righteousness" (verse 2)? How does Jesus' death on the cross reveal his righteousness even more fully?

The Text in the Bigger Story

Read Matthew 21:1-11 about Jesus' triumphal entry into Jerusalem.

21 As they approached Jerusalem and came to Bethphage on the Mount of Olives, Jesus sent two disciples, 2 saying to them, "Go to the village ahead of you, and at once you will find a donkey tied there, with her colt by her. Untie them and bring them to me. 3 If anyone says anything to you, say that the Lord needs them, and he will send them right away."

4 This took place to fulfill what was spoken through the prophet:

> 5 "Say to Daughter Zion,
> 'See, your king comes to you,
> gentle and riding on a donkey,
> and on a colt, the foal of a donkey.'"

⁶ The disciples went and did as Jesus had instructed them. ⁷ They brought the donkey and the colt and placed their cloaks on them for Jesus to sit on. ⁸ A very large crowd spread their cloaks on the road, while others cut branches from the trees and spread them on the road. ⁹ The crowds that went ahead of him and those that followed shouted,

> "Hosanna to the Son of David!"
> "Blessed is he who comes in the name of the Lord!"
> "Hosanna in the highest heaven!"

¹⁰ When Jesus entered Jerusalem, the whole city was stirred and asked, "Who is this?"

¹¹ The crowds answered, "This is Jesus, the prophet from Nazareth in Galilee."

4. In the psalm and in Matthew 21, we notice the resulting—and loud—worship of the glorious God who is worthy of praise because of his authority. When you consider praising God out loud, either to other Christians or to those who do not identify as Christians, what prompts your praise? What prompted the praise of the crowd in Matthew 21?

Jesus Completing the Story

5. In Psalm 98:7-9 all of nature joins humanity in praising God. How will God's salvation make things right, so that both mankind and all creation are free to live as God originally intended?

Living Out the Story

6. Psalm 98 begins with a command to sing and ends with a picture of all creation singing together. As you journey through the season of Lent, what are some of the "marvelous things" you have experienced in your reflection on Jesus' life and death? How might you engage others in your rejoicing?

PRAYER

Throughout Lent we will practice meditation on the psalm we are studying, using the following steps:

❍ One group member reads Psalm 98 out loud.

❍ Allow 5 minutes for silent reflection on the psalm, considering a word, phrase or verse that captured your mind or attention. Prayerfully reflect on it before God and meditate on the obstacles that prevent you from fully believing or obeying God.

❍ Re-read the psalm out loud once more, with two or more group members facilitating the oral reading.

❍ Go around the group, with each person sharing the one phrase that captured their thinking, with no additional commentary provided, simply the biblical text that was meaningful to them.

Close in prayer, giving thanks for the things God has taught you during the study of the psalm.

Prayer for the King

SCRIPTURE

Psalm 110 (NIV)

¹ The LORD says to my LORD:
  "Sit at my right hand
    until I make your enemies
    a footstool for your feet."

² The LORD will extend your mighty scepter from Zion, saying,
    "Rule in the midst of your enemies!"
³ Your troops will be willing
    on your day of battle.
Arrayed in holy splendor,
    your young men will come to you
    like dew from the morning's womb.

⁴ The LORD has sworn
    and will not change his mind:
"You are a priest forever,
    in the order of Melchizedek."

⁵ The LORD is at your right hand;
    he will crush kings on the day of his wrath.
⁶ He will judge the nations, heaping up the dead
    and crushing the rulers of the whole earth.
⁷ He will drink from a brook along the way,
    and so he will lift his head high.

DISCUSSION

Goal of This Study: The goal of this study is to acknowledge Jesus as the Messiah–our true king and priest—and to realize the resulting assurance and courage to fight every spiritual battle.

Background Information: We are entering the sixth week of Lent, which includes Palm Sunday. Remember that Lent is a season of joyful repentance because the goal is to bring renewal to our lives. Lent corresponds to Jesus' time in the wilderness, where he hungered and thirsted for 40 days. We are studying specific psalms that help us in times of difficulty and spiritual dissonance.

This week we will explore Psalm 110, considered to be a messianic or royal psalm, in which the writer is looking forward to the coming of the promised messianic king. The Old Testament anticipates a great ruler in the line of King David whose reign would last forever. This is important in helping us understand Jesus' kingship, and it is the most often quoted text in the New Testament. As a messianic psalm it predicts the divinity, priesthood and victories of the messiah, one person who is both human and divine. Studying this psalm in conjunction with Jesus' triumphal entry into Jerusalem, when the people thought he would be their earthly king, will help us reflect on Jesus as our ultimate king and eternal priest.

The Text

1. **The Israelites were looking forward to a messiah-king who would usher in God's reign. Describe what kind of king this psalm depicts (verses 1-3). Does Jesus fulfill these qualities? If so, how?**

2. Unlike the Israelites, most modern people do not want someone else ruling their lives, as a king would necessarily do. How might Jesus as the messiah-king change your life and the lives of those around you today?

The Text in the Bigger Story

Read Matthew 21:1-11 again this week (see page 39-40), about Jesus' triumphal entry into Jerusalem, along with Zechariah 9:9.

Rejoice greatly, Daughter Zion!
  Shout, Daughter Jerusalem!
See, your king comes to you,
  righteous and victorious,
lowly and riding on a donkey,
  on a colt, the foal of a donkey.

3. Psalm 110 and Matthew 21 depict very different entries of the king. What are the most striking contrasts between the two royal entries described?

Jesus Completing the Story

4. Though Jesus, the messiah-king, came in his first coming as the meek suffering servant, Psalm 110 points to his second coming in which he will have final victory over every enemy. Why can it be difficult to believe this will be true, both culturally and personally? In what ways do you need to trust him to work?

Living Out the Story

5. What difference would it make in your life if you regularly experienced Jesus as your priest and king?

6. Looking back on this study, what do you need to repent of in order to follow Jesus, our powerful king and priest? How can the group pray for you about this?

PRAYER

Throughout Lent we will practice meditation on the psalm we are studying, using the following steps:

- ● One group member reads Psalm 110 out loud.

- ● Allow 5 minutes for silent reflection on the psalm, considering a word, phrase or verse that captured your mind or attention. Prayerfully reflect on it before God and meditate on the obstacles that prevent you from fully believing or obeying God.

- ● Re-read the psalm out loud once more, with two or more group members facilitating the oral reading.

- ● Go around the group, with each person sharing the one phrase that captured their thinking, with no additional commentary provided, simply the biblical text that was meaningful to them.

Close in prayer, giving thanks for the things God has taught you during the study of the psalm.

Prayer for Security

SCRIPTURE

Psalm 16 (NIV)

¹ Keep me safe, my God,
    for in you I take refuge.
² I say to the LORD, "You are my LORD;
    apart from you I have no good thing."
³ I say of the holy people who are in the land,
    "They are the noble ones in whom is all my delight."
⁴ Those who run after other gods will suffer more and more.
    I will not pour out libations of blood to such gods
    or take up their names on my lips.

⁵ LORD, you alone are my portion and my cup;
    you make my lot secure.
⁶ The boundary lines have fallen for me in pleasant places;
    surely I have a delightful inheritance.
⁷ I will praise the LORD, who counsels me;
    even at night my heart instructs me.
⁸ I keep my eyes always on the LORD.
    With him at my right hand, I will not be shaken.

⁹ Therefore my heart is glad and my tongue rejoices;
    my body also will rest secure,
¹⁰ because you will not abandon me to the realm of the dead,
    nor will you let your faithful one see decay.
¹¹ You make known to me the path of life;
    you will fill me with joy in your presence,
    with eternal pleasures at your right hand.

DISCUSSION

Goal of This Study: The goal of this study is to better understand how the resurrection of Jesus informs every part of our lives today, especially our most pressing fears of security and mortality.

Background Information: During the season of Lent, we have used the Psalms to guide us in spiritual reflection and self-examination. There has been a focus on repentance (Psalm 32), as well as a focus on rejoicing in hope (Psalm 98). And in this study we realize that all of this—our repenting and our rejoicing— is made possible because Jesus fought and defeated death on that first Easter Sunday.

As we turn from the season of Lent to the celebration of Easter, we turn to Psalm 16. Appropriately, this psalm was quoted by the apostle Peter, in one of his first sermons, to prove Jesus' bodily resurrection (Acts 2:22-33).

This psalm begins with David's cry to God for safety (v. 1) and culminates with David's confidence that God can keep him safe from all evil, even from death itself (v. 10).[2] Though David's confidence in God's ability to keep him safe was rightly rooted in God's demonstrated faithfulness throughout the Old Testament, we as Christian believers possess an even greater confidence. All of God's covenant promises and prophetic declarations about a messiah-savior have been fulfilled in the centerpiece of history we celebrate at Easter!

---

[2] See Tremper Longman, *Psalms: An Introduction and Commentary* (Downers Grove, Ill: Intervarsity Press, 2014), 103-7.

The Text

1. In the opening line, David cries out to God, asking to be kept safe. According to the text, what is threatening David? How does your need for safety parallel that of David?

2. According to Psalm 16:5, what words does David use to describe God? What do you think those images suggest?

3. According to Psalm 16:6-7, what has God done for David? In what ways would knowing God like this influence the way you see your life?

The Text in the Bigger Story

Read together Acts 2:22-33.

22 "Fellow Israelites, listen to this: Jesus of Nazareth was a man accredited by God to you by miracles, wonders and signs, which God did among you through him, as you yourselves know.
23 This man was handed over to you by God's deliberate plan and foreknowledge; and you, with the help of wicked men, put him to death by nailing him to the cross. 24 But God raised him from the dead, freeing him from the agony of death, because it was impossible for death to keep its hold on him. 25 David said about him:

> "'I saw the Lord always before me.
>   Because he is at my right hand,
>   I will not be shaken.
> 26 Therefore my heart is glad and my tongue rejoices;
>   my body also will rest in hope,
> 27 because you will not abandon me to the realm of the dead,
>   you will not let your holy one see decay.
> 28 You have made known to me the paths of life;
>   you will fill me with joy in your presence.'

29 "Fellow Israelites, I can tell you confidently that the patriarch David died and was buried, and his tomb is here to this day.
30 But he was a prophet and knew that God had promised him on oath that he would place one of his descendants on his throne.
31 Seeing what was to come, he spoke of the resurrection of the Messiah, that he was not abandoned to the realm of the dead, nor did his body see decay. 32 God has raised this Jesus to life, and we are all witnesses of it. 33 Exalted to the right hand of God, he has received from the Father the promised Holy Spirit and has poured out what you now see and hear.

4. In Acts 2 the apostle Peter interprets Psalm 16 to be looking forward to Jesus' resurrection. Why is it important that Peter quotes this particular psalm?

Jesus Completing the Story

5. What can we learn about Peter using this text in his first recorded sermon? What does this tell us about how the early Christians read Scripture?

Living Out the Story

6. In his book *Miracles*, C.S. Lewis wrote about Jesus' resurrection saying, "[Jesus] has met, fought, and beaten the King of Death. Everything is different because he has done so."[3] If it's true that Jesus was raised from the dead, how should your life be different? How is the whole world different?

---

[3] C.S. Lewis, *Miracles* (New York: Harper, 2000), 237.

PRAYER

Throughout Lent we will practice meditation on the psalm we are studying, using the following steps:

○ One group member reads Psalm 16 out loud.

○ Allow 5 minutes for silent reflection on the psalm, considering a word, phrase or verse that captured your mind or attention. Prayerfully reflect on it before God and meditate on the obstacles that prevent you from fully believing or obeying God.

○ Re-read the psalm out loud once more, with two or more group members facilitating the oral reading.

○ Go around the group, with each person sharing the one phrase that captured their thinking, with no additional commentary provided, simply the biblical text that was meaningful to them.

Following this, take a longer time to pray, giving thanks for all the things God has brought to light during the study of these psalms and the season of Lent. Praise him for his power displayed at Easter! Praise him for his glorious kingdom, which is advancing and will culminate in the new heavens and new earth, where there will be no more death:

> Then I saw "a new heaven and a new earth," for the first heaven and the first earth had passed away, and there was no longer any sea. ² I saw the Holy City, the new Jerusalem, coming down out of heaven from God, prepared as a bride beautifully dressed for her husband. ³ And I heard a loud voice from the throne saying, "Look! God's dwelling place is now among the people, and he will dwell with them. They will be his people, and God himself will be with them and be their God. ⁴ 'He will wipe every tear from their eyes. There will be no more death' or mourning or crying or pain, for the old order of things has passed away" (Revelation 21:1-4).

A JOURNEY THROUGH LENT
Reflecting on Christ's Sacrifice for Us

• LEADER'S NOTES •

INSTRUCTIONS TO LEADERS

This guide is provided only as a basic framework. The goal of each lesson is not to master the material or answer all the questions, but to grow in our knowledge of Jesus and his teachings and to develop deeper relationships with one another.

That being said, you, as the leader, should review the lesson in advance with the goal of choosing the best discussion questions for your particular group. Feel free to insert your own community-building "ice breaker" question at the start of each lesson, one that aligns itself with the key principles of the lesson and will engage your group members. Feel free to pick and choose from the menu of discussion questions the ones that are best suited for your particular group. You may also want to customize the Living Out the Story questions and prayers.

We trust that you and your group members will grow together in your knowledge and appreciation of all that Jesus has accomplished for us at the cross. As you journey through Lent, may your spiritual senses be awakened to more vividly comprehend his "incomparably great power for us who believe and may you experience this resurrection power in your life as we journey toward the day of seeing Christ seated "in the heavenly realms" (Ephesians 1:19-20).

STUDY #1
Prayer of Confession

Psalm 32
See page 7

---

1. Overall, the psalm rejoices in forgiveness and the joy it brings. But first, what do verses 3 and 4 tell us about sin and its consequences? Does this ring true to your experience?

The goal of this question is to reflect on the dangers and consequences of sin and to realize that while sin is ultimately against God, it also harms us. Sin and guilt often bear psychological and emotional consequences, leading to a deep "groaning" (v. 3). Indeed, one psychiatrist is known to have said, "I could dismiss half my patients tomorrow, if I could assure them that they were forgiven."

Our failure to acknowledge and confess sin can also include physical consequences. The psalmist's body is "wasting away" (v. 3) and his "strength is sapped" (v. 4). It is imperative we realize that God has set up the world in such a way that when we disregard his commands, we are simultaneously harming ourselves. Sin harms us. Many people will have experienced how debilitating guilt can be. It breaks our fellowship with God. It can lead to self-loathing. Many will also have firsthand experience of how it has damaged relationships. Sin is about more than "going against the grain" of the universe, but it is not less than that.

2. What obstacles do we face in believing that sin brings harm to us? Where have you personally encountered difficulty believing that sin is destructive?

First, there is the pleasure that sin offers. One Puritan writer said that "Satan shows us the bait and hides the hook." The attractiveness of the bait initially allures us and blinds us to the consequences. Sometimes it takes us a while to see the negative consequences of disobeying God. At other times, we blind ourselves to the consequences. In still other instances, we never see the negative consequences in this life at all. In those cases, we are especially called on to take God at his word. We aren't convinced that we will stand before the judgment seat of God at the end of our lives. This is the most significant long-term consequence of sin. If we do believe in a final judgment, we might be prone to believe that we aren't so bad and God would never condemn us.

3. What is involved in genuine repentance, according to verse 5?

Genuine repentance involves seeing our sin primarily as an offense against God and turning away from it out of love for God. Genuine repentance involves honesty about our sin before God. "I did not cover up my iniquity" (v. 5). We no longer try to hide it, justify it, or blame others for it. Genuine repentance involves confessing our sin and naming it. Genuine repentance acknowledges that our actions are ultimately against God, not just other people. The psalmist confesses his transgressions "to the Lord," with the understanding that it was an action against him. Genuine repentance involves not simply or even primarily being sorry, but a complete change in behavior. The word "transgression" involves going over a boundary set by God. To acknowledge that we have transgressed against God and to repent implies turning around from that behavior and back to God and his standards.

4. Remorse or fear may lead to change because we want to avoid the consequences of a wrong behavior. Why is true repentance done out of love for God and a desire to avoid grieving him more appropriate and effective?

While repentance does involve seeing the danger of sin, if we go no further than that, our confession is nothing but a calculated, self-interested way to avoid pain. We have simply decided sin was not worth it, in a sort of spiritual cost-benefit analysis. Our hearts, however, are seldom changed by a cost-benefit analysis. We may have temporarily restrained our desires, but our hearts are not changed; we would still engage in the behavior if we could get away with it without experiencing the consequences. We don't see the inherent ugliness of the behavior and the offense it is to God, and so our hearts do not turn from it.

True repentance sees sin as first and foremost against God. Outward consequences aren't the first concern of true repentance. The consequence that matters is that we have grieved God, who both created us and loves us. Repentance done out of love for God understands that our relationship with God is the central issue. Our friendship with God is what motivates and drives us. True repentance brings about a real change in heart. It involves a new hatred of sin as sin and not simply a hatred of its consequences. It also desires a renewed relationship with God. We see the preciousness of that relationship and don't want to put it in jeopardy. We no longer treat sin casually or lightly.

The Text in the Bigger Story   (5-10 minutes)

Read Romans 4:4-12 with Psalm 32 in mind.

Paul, in quoting from Psalm 32 in his letter to the Romans, interprets the psalm to include the fact that God credits righteousness to the one whose sins are covered. In other words, God not only removes sin, but also imputes righteousness, so that we receive not simply a blank slate but a new record of righteousness.

5. What does the language of Psalm 32 (and quoted in Romans 4) teach us about what is involved in the wonderful gift of forgiveness?

The goal of this question is to understand the depths and riches of what is entailed in God's forgiveness of us and how this can inform not just our actions but also renew our hearts.

The concept of forgiveness conveys rich meaning for us. The word "forgive" means to lift something up and throw it away or let it go. The word "cover" conveys the idea that though something is still there, we are not letting it affect us. Though sin and ugliness are still present in our lives, God covers it so that his attention is taken away from it as he relates to us. "Does not count against us" is language that is legal in nature. It means he does not treat us as sinners. We are acquitted rather than condemned.

A potential follow up question: How does this help you or challenge you regarding your own practice of forgiving others?

Jesus Completing the Story   (5-10 minutes)

6. How does the sacrificial death of Jesus enrich our understanding of God's forgiveness and lead us to a place of genuine heartfelt and joyful repentance?

On the one hand, the cross helps us see the depths of our sin. So horrific is our sin that it required the death of God's Son to pay for it. On the other hand, the cross helps us to see the depths of God's love. God, in

Christ and at great cost to himself, was willing to give his very life for us. He loves us so much that he did not spare his own son!

As shown in Romans 4, God not only removes sin, but also imputes righteousness; we get not simply a blank slate, but Christ's record of righteousness. When we understand and allow this truth to penetrate deeply into our hearts—the extravagance of God in not only removing sin from us but also crediting righteousness to us—we are led to a joy and gratitude that become the driving force and motivation of the Christian life. We find ourselves wanting to turn from sin and to live for Jesus fully. Sin gets cut off at the root! While the psalmist could assent to a "clean spirit" (Psalm 51), we have the full understanding of just what it took for God to forgive us! Even more than the psalmist, we can "be glad in the LORD, and rejoice...and shout for joy, all you upright in heart!" (Psalm 32:11).

Living Out the Story   (15-20 minutes)

The following are open-ended questions to encourage gospel application and group participation.

7. **In what ways do we fail to own our sin and what effect does that have on us?**

8. **Take a moment to consider a recurring sin in your life. What is at the root of that sin? How can you begin to cut off that sin at the root?**

As the facilitator, be prepared in advance to answer this question with a personal example. It should also be noted that getting to the root of recurring sins is difficult, requiring time and analysis. It also requires living in faithful, helpful community. Encourage your group to allow others to speak into their hidden areas to help expose blind spots.

Additional Question   (to use if time allows)

In verses 9 and 10, God offers wisdom to the readers of the psalm. What does the example of the mule suggest about the difference between those who behave wickedly and those who behave righteously? How do we get to the place where we are numbered among the righteous?

The horse and mule have no willingness to go in a particular direction. They have to be coerced and dragged! Forces outside of them must do the controlling since there is no internal willingness. Unfortunately, many Christians live like this. It is a joyless and exhausting approach to the Christian life. They are driven by either consequences ("God will punish me if I don't obey him") or rewards ("God will only love me if I obey him"). This is essentially moralism, and it is a sub-Christian way to live. This approach is contrasted with those who trust in God's unfailing love, who obey simply because they love the one who has extravagantly initiated love. "We love him because he first loved us" (1 John 4:19).

STUDY #2
Prayer of Seeking

Psalm 34
See page 15

The Text	(15-20 minutes)

1. Having experienced great suffering, David now urges the afflicted to do what he did: cry out to God and experience his protection and peace (verses 1-3). How have you experienced suffering? Where did you turn in your suffering?

The goal of this question is to have the group open up about past suffering and to recognize patterns of handling suffering, as well as learn how to handle suffering wisely.

Suffering is inevitable. Though we work and plan for success and security, we see here that suffering, our own or that of those close to us, is sure to come. In fact, we find warning of this exact thing in Ecclesiastes 12:1, "Look to the Lord in the days of your youth before the days of trouble come." Another way of saying this is: "Learn now that the Lord is trustworthy, because trials are coming and with it suffering." Since suffering is universal, many are in the midst of life-changing troubles now. David says that when he turned to God, his suffering was used as an opportunity to grow in grace and not in bitterness.

In times of suffering we can become self-absorbed; indeed, it is hard not to. The blessings and joys of others, in those we love, don't touch us if we are focused on our misery and our fears.

It is easy to become isolated. But the psalm begins with an invitation to exalt God and praise him in community "together" (v. 3).

In times of suffering, we choose to either glorify God in the midst of our situation, or not. Look to Hosea 7:14: "They do not cry out to me from their hearts but wail about their beds." This means that when we are hurting we can do one of two things, either "cry on our bed or cry to the

Lord."[4] David urges us to not turn inward, but to call out to God (v. 6), so that we may rejoice "at all times."

Most of us rejoice when things go well or according to our plan. David, however, charges the reader to bless the Lord "at all times" even during days of trouble. This is a way to say that we must remain thankful, expectant, and dependent on God no matter the circumstances. As Elisabeth Elliot said, "The key to happiness is Christ in me, not me in a different set of circumstances."

2. David attests that when we seek God in these times, we can experience deliverance and liberation from the power of suffering in our lives (verses 4-7). As a group, consider aloud what deliverance, liberation and even protection from suffering might look like?

If you know the story of David, then you know that suffering in his life was a constant. Therefore, when David talks of deliverance and liberation, he can't mean our lives will now be impervious to heartache or trials. He must mean that in seeking (and finding) God we are given a new perspective on our condition, one that injects life and hope into our circumstances rather than death and despair.

In these verses David says that he relied on the Lord during trouble and he was not put to shame (v. 5), meaning, he was not disappointed. Though his circumstances may not have changed, his viewpoint did. The angel of the Lord protected him (v. 7). The "angel of the Lord" in the Old Testament is God himself come down to earth in a form that enables him to come near to rescue without destroying. This is the pre-incarnate Son of God, Jesus.

David has the audacity to say that not only will you experience the glory of God in your innermost being, but also others will notice (v. 5). You will be radiant to others in the midst of dark times! "Radiant" is a Hebrew word that in Isaiah 60:5 describes a mother's face when she sees her children, but in Exodus 34:29 and 2 Corinthians 3:18 it refers to Moses' face shining as he comes down from having met with God. According to one commentator, "Radiance is delight but also glory: a transformation of the whole person."[5]

4   Edward Welch, *Depression: Looking Up from the Stubborn Darkness* (Greensboro, NC: New Growth Press, 2011), 43.
5   Derek Kidner, *Psalms: Old Testament Commentary* (Carol Stream, Ill: Tyndale House Publishers, 1973), 157.

3. **God promises through David that when you take refuge in him you will lack "no good thing." Many of us know this in our head, yet in our daily lives we seek less reliable sources for satisfaction or security. Why is it so hard to believe that in God we will lack nothing we really need? How might David's language here move us to greater degrees of trust and pleasure in God?**

Tasting the goodness of God is an invitation to move beyond mere knowledge to actual experience. No one has explained this better than Jonathan Edwards with his illustration of honey:

> Thus there is a difference between having an opinion, that God is holy and gracious, and having a sense of the loveliness and beauty of that holiness and grace. There is a difference between having a rational judgment that honey is sweet, and having a sense of its sweetness. A man may have the former, that knows not how honey tastes; but a man cannot have the latter unless he has an idea of the taste of honey in his mind.[6]

The Text in the Bigger Story   (5-10 minutes)

Read together Romans 8:1,18-37.

Romans 8:1 begins with the echo of the last verse of Psalm 34, and it helps to read them back to back: "The Lord will rescue his servants; no one who takes refuge in him will be condemned...There is therefore now no condemnation for those who are in Christ Jesus." Although the psalmist finds comfort in who God is, we receive greater comfort from what God has done for us in Jesus Christ. Romans 8 goes on to depict the reality of suffering, as well as God's purposes for allowing suffering in our lives.

4. **From Genesis to Revelation, the Bible reveals God's plan to bring creation from suffering into glory. According to Romans 8, what can we learn about our own suffering?**

The goal of this question is to allow group members to consider the theology of suffering and biblical responses to it. According to both the psalmist David (Psalm 32) and the Apostle Paul (Romans 8), we should expect suffering. Although our modern Western culture has influenced us to protect against suffering and insure against all calamity, suffering is a normal part of life and has much to offer—the opportunity to learn

---

[6] Jonathan Edwards in his sermon "A Divine and Supernatural Light, Immediately Imparted to the Soul by the Spirit of God, Shown to be Both Scriptural and Rational Doctrine" preached at Northampton in 1734.

patience (Romans 8:25), a deeper prayer life (8:26), a greater sense of God's call and purpose (8:28), unmovable hope and resolve (8:37-38).

Jesus Completing the Story   (5-10 minutes)

5. What do we learn about our suffering and our ability to trust God in light of Jesus' death on the cross?

Jesus demonstrates his willingness to suffer alongside us, and ultimately in our place. Jesus experiences the opposite of glory so that David—and you and I—could experience it now and in the future. David in his suffering called out to God, and the Lord answered. Yet, in Matthew 27:46, Jesus on the cross experiences the opposite. Christ calls out to his Father, "My God, my God, why has thou forsaken me?" but there is no answer.

Verse 20 is notable for its reference to Jesus. It is quoted in John 19:36, as being fulfilled when Jesus died before his executioners could break his legs to hasten his death. However, just reading this psalm we would more naturally think that this was a promise of protection, that nothing bad, not even a broken leg, will happen to us. From our New Testament vantage point, however, we see that although God did protect Jesus from having broken legs, he also allowed him to be crucified—not exactly a "get out of suffering" promise.

The solution to this puzzle is in verse 22, where it says that God will rescue his servants. Jesus was protected, as we are, but sometimes that rescue from suffering comes on the far side of resurrection, not on this side of it.

We trust God will rescue his servants because he himself became the servant who suffered that we might find refuge in him. Dr. Timothy Keller writes, "Suffering is unbearable if you aren't certain that God is for you and with you."[7] But because of the cross you can be sure: "Jesus lost all his glory so that we could be clothed in it. He was shut out so we could get access. He was bound, nailed, so that we could be free. He was cast out so we could approach. And Jesus took away the only kind of suffering that can really destroy you: that is being cast away from God. He took it so that now all suffering that comes into your life will only make you great. A lump of coal under pressure becomes a diamond. And the suffering of a person in Christ only turns you into somebody gorgeous."[8]

---

[7] Timothy J. Keller, *Walking With God Through Pain and Suffering* (New York: Penguin Publishing Group, 2015), 58.

[8] Ibid., 180-181.

Living Out the Story   (15-20 minutes)

6. How does Christianity uniquely redeem our suffering?

The goal of this question is to see how a Christian understands suffering and what that means not only for our lives but also for those around us. In an impersonal world, both the joys and ills of life hold no value. Therefore, suffering has no meaning and is only an interruption in life. Yet, this is not the case with Christianity. Because Christianity believes in a universe created by a personal God who seeks to restore his creation, both delightful and difficult seasons are viewed as opportunities to bless him for his love and faithfulness. "Christianity teaches that, contra fatalism, suffering is overwhelming; contra Buddhism, suffering is real; contra karma, suffering is often unfair; but contra secularism, suffering is meaningful. There is a purpose to it, and if faced rightly, it can drive us like a nail deep into the love of God and into more stability and spiritual power than you can imagine."[9]

Additional Question   (to use if time allows)

What does "fear of the Lord" mean? How might that "fear" be a good and helpful way to nurture holiness in our daily life?

Fear of God is one of the richest and most basic concepts of biblical theology. The fear of God is not merely a selfish fear of punishment, but the awe and trembling fear of those who have such a grasp of God's greatness and so much love for him that they are afraid of dishonoring and grieving him. It means to know him with mind and heart and treat him as supremely valuable.

If you fear God—not merely believe in or obey him but know, love and treat him as supremely important—then you will "lack no good thing." That means not that you will get everything you want, but you will have everything you need. "It is not an empty promise of affluence but an assurance of his responsible care."[10] John Newton, who was no stranger to suffering, said, "Everything is needful that he sends; nothing can be needful that he withholds."

---

[9] Ibid., 30.
[10] Derek Kidner, *Psalms: Old Testament Commentary* (Carol Stream, Ill: Tyndale House Publishers, 1973), 158.

STUDY #3
Prayer of Thirst

Psalms 42-43
See page 23

The Text   (15-20 minutes)

1. Describe what the psalmist is experiencing and feeling, focusing primarily on Psalm 42:1-5. When do you tend to think or feel this way?

The goal of this question is to understand the nature of spiritually dry times for the psalmist and for ourselves. Begin by considering the emotions of the psalmist, and conclude this first question by inviting group members to share how and when they experience this common condition of spiritual dissonance. Allow people to share honestly from their experiences.

First, he begins by lamenting, "My soul thirsts for God" (42:1), describing his condition as severe spiritual dryness or drought. The condition is conveyed by the image of a deer dying of thirst (42:1). Deer are creatures of instinct and ones that drink constantly; deer would be parched and deeply thirsty if there were a drought. The psalmist is conveying his spiritual dryness as drought, a drying up of necessary resources.

The word "downcast" occurs three times in 42:5, 42:11 and 43:5; it is a general word for being despondent or depressed. The question, "Where can I go and meet with God?" has several possible implications. Perhaps he is unable to worship God in the temple for which he longs, as is implied by "the face," or presence, of God (v. 3b). Or perhaps he lacks an experience of God; the psalmist is bemoaning the loss of God's reality to his soul. When he says, "Where is God?" he is not talking intellectually (as some skeptics do); he is not saying that he doesn't believe in him, but rather that he cannot feel the living God. He lacks the joy he used to have in worship.

Ask group members to share their experiences of spiritual dryness or distance from God. Be prepared to acknowledge your own experiences.

2. In this passage, what do you see that might have triggered his hopelessness? What don't you see? Discuss in your group other factors for spiritual apathy that are not in this psalm.

The goal of this question is to consider what we can learn about asking God in prayer from the content (what) and manner (how) of the psalmist's prayers.

Disruption of community and worship. The author appears to have been moved some distance from the temple and the congregation of people who worshiped there. He remembers having gone to the house of God with the multitude (42:4), but now he lives near the mountains of Hermon and Mizar (42:6). This does not mean that he can't pray or experience God where he is, but it is worshiping in community that is normative, a gift from God, and apart from it, all is not as it should be.

Living in a skeptical, spiritually hostile environment. The author is being worn down by those who question the reality or the power of the biblical God. They continually ask him, "Where is your God?" (42:3,10).

Two factors that are not mentioned anywhere in these psalms are sin and major tragedy. Although there is often a loss of fellowship with God that stems from guilt over sin, there is no confession of sin mentioned in these psalms. The dryness that is experienced here is not the result of bad conscience. Secondly, though the word "enemy" is mentioned twice, it is not referring to specific combative enemies, which implies he is not fleeing for his life. Therefore, this is not a case where the ways of God become inscrutable or seemingly unjust to even the faithful.

3. One of the breakthroughs in prayer is to learn how to lament honestly and rightly. What did the psalmist do to remedy his downcast heart?

He pours out his soul (42:1-4). The psalmist exposes his inner self to God in prayer. He is crying, longing, reflecting and remembering, all before God. It could be called the ancient and healthy version of what is sometimes now called "getting in touch with one's feelings." It means to look honestly at your doubts, desires, fears, and hopes. It is not giving up, but praying in a sustained, focused way, even when the feelings do not immediately change.

He honestly talks to himself (42:5,11 and 43:5). Perhaps the most remarkable thing we see in the psalm is that the psalmist does not only talk to God, but he speaks to himself. He preaches to his soul. This is a very critical skill, as noted by D. Martyn Lloyd-Jones:

The first thing we have to learn is what the Psalmist learned, that we must learn to take ourselves in hand...He is talking to himself, he is addressing himself...We must talk to ourselves instead of allowing "ourselves" to talk to us. This is the very essence of wisdom in this matter. Have you realized that so much of the unhappiness in your life is due to the fact you are listening to yourself instead of talking to yourself?...So this man stands up and says: "Self, listen for a moment..." Then you must go on to remind yourself of who God is, and what God is and what God has done and what God has pledged himself to do....Then end on this great note: defy yourself, and defy other people, and defy the devil and the whole world, and say with the man, "I shall yet praise Him...for he is my God."[11]

He analyzes his hopes. He says, "Why are you cast down?" and then immediately exhorts his soul with "put your hope in God." This must mean that the reason he is cast down is that he has not put his hope in God but rather in something else—his record or people's acclaim or changed circumstances. Though spiritual dissonance is not the direct result of sin, it usually reveals to us inordinate loves and false hopes.

He remembers times when he worshiped with joy. At the heart of the psalmist's predicament is an awareness of the absence of God, and through the tool of memory, he is determined to attempt to dispel that sense of absence and distance. He meditates on God's love at night (42:5b). He realizes that the waves of despair he is experiencing are "your" waves (42:7), in accordance with God's sovereign plans. Even when he questions God, he calls him "my Rock" (42:9) and "my stronghold." He is meditating on God's name, attributes, and how God has shown him love throughout his life (43:2). He changes his lament to prayer (43:1-5). He calls on God to do something, and though all his circumstances have not changed, he has made progress in his spiritual journey.

The Text in the Bigger Story   (5-10 minutes)

Read together Mark 15:24-39.

This psalm can be viewed through the lens of the greatest suffering of all time—from the viewpoint of Jesus on the cross: "My bones suffer mortal agony as my foes taunt me, saying to me all day long, 'Where is your God?'" (Psalm 42:10). As a group, read reflectively Mark's narrative of Jesus' crucifixion.

---

[11] D. Martyn Lloyd-Jones, *Spiritual Depression: Its Causes and Its Cure* (London: HarperCollins Publishers, 1965). 20-21.

4. Compare and contrast the mocking of the psalmist and the mocking of Christ on the cross. Why is the psalmist being mocked? Why is Jesus being mocked?

The psalmist seems to be experiencing mocking because he worships God, as opposed to those around him who worship other gods. It appears that the psalmist has been moved some distance from the temple and the congregation of people that worshiped there. He remembers having gone to the house of God with the multitude (42:4), but now he lives near the mountains of Hermon and Mizar (42:6).

Jesus is being mocked by the very ones who had exultantly praised him just a week before when he entered Jerusalem. Their hostility is palpable and echoes the taunts of the psalmist's tormentors: "And those who passed by derided him, wagging their heads and saying, 'Aha! You who would destroy the temple and rebuild it in three days, save yourself, and come down from the cross!'" (Mark 15:29-30).

Jesus Completing the Story   (5-10 minutes)

5. How can Jesus' thirsting and experience of being forsaken for you change you, so that you seek hope and satisfaction in him?

Jesus experienced the ultimate abandonment on the cross, when he was separated from the Father, whom he had been with in perfect communion since before the dawn of time. He was forsaken by God so that we would never have to be, so that we could be brought near and called God's children: "For it was fitting that he, for whom and by whom all things exist, in bringing many sons to glory, should make the founder of their salvation perfect through suffering" (Hebrews 2:10).

The book of Hebrews goes on to tell us that it was because of the joy set before him that Jesus could endure the agony of the cross (Hebrews 12:2). We are that joy for which he endured.

Take a minute as a group to consider how Jesus can understand the times when you feel like God is absent.

Living Out the Story   (15-20 minutes)

6. What would it look like for you to hope in God in the midst of a current disturbing time? How can your community help each other?

Give your group some time to share honestly with each other. Pray as they are sharing that they could solidly encourage each other to put their hope in Christ.

After each expression of grief and pain, the refrain, "Put your hope in God" holds out the possibility of healing and future praise. Indeed each section moves upward, so we see the psalmist move from dark despair to confidence. This gives us hope for our own times of dryness. And it reveals that the process is indeed just that, a gradual process with many twists and turns.

Additional Questions   (to use if time allows)

Can we prevent or avoid dry times? Why or why not?

Allow the group to discuss their opinions on this question. Since everyone will experience lack of hope at times in his or her life, have the group discuss this reality.

It's true that spiritual emptiness can result from our seeking happiness and identity from things other than God. In this case, repentance often is the first step out of a season of spiritual apathy. It is also true, however, that low seasons just come, not as a result of sin or circumstance, but as a part of the life of every Christian. God can use these seasons to show us our complete dependence upon him alone. Moreover, these spells of spiritual dryness can serve to foster a greater hunger for God himself, rather than seeking God for the blessings he gives.

Where do you tend to turn when times are hard?

Let your group honestly engage with their thoughts and each other about the alternate sources of hope we turn to during times of suffering.

75

STUDY #4
Prayer of Rest

Psalm 91
See page 31

See page 31

The Text   (15-20 minutes)

1. Throughout the psalm the writer assumes that people need rest from the stresses and troubles of life. How do you identify with that need?

In order to have a real conversation about the rest that God provides, we need to first admit our need for rest. This question offers a chance for your group to do that. You don't need to spend a lot of time here—just get people engaged and opening up.

2. The first four verses of Psalm 91 establish the foundational principle that God protects his loved ones. Consider the descriptions that the psalmist uses in verses 1 to 4, and envision together what protection from God is like. How is God a defense and rest to those who trust him?

The following words are used to describe our safety in the Almighty:

Shelter and shadow (v. 1). The word for "shadow" in this verse means literally "shade." In that time and place, the hot sun could often be deadly. Shade was a refreshing and life-giving protection from the sun's rays. God is our protection from the arrows of daily life when we sit in the shade of his presence and provision.

Refuge and fortress (v. 2). Places of refuge and fortress are areas of security and peace in the midst of attack. In the Old Testament, God ordained the building of "cities of refuge" to which people could flee if pursued after causing the death of someone. They received shelter and mercy (see Numbers 35 and 1 Chronicles 6). It is likely that the psalmist has this is mind when he describes God as a shelter, a place to seek refuge from imminent threats. God himself is our place of security when daily stresses and life-altering troubles come.

A covering (v. 4). The phrase "cover you with his feathers" evokes the image of a mother bird protecting and providing for its young. The mother eagle image is also used in Deuteronomy 32:10-11, where it says, "he guarded him [Israel] as the apple of his eye, like an eagle that...hovers over its young, that spreads its wings to catch them and carries them aloft." The image of God as a mother bird reinforces the fact that our God is not a remote, distant parent. Moreover, the comparison to a majestic eagle conveys power and loftiness with tenderness and support for weakness—a picture of grace.

Shield and rampart (v. 4). This military image indicates an unyielding strength or armor that will be a strong defense in battle against attacking foes.

3. **The psalmist writes bold statements concerning protection God provides for those who trust in him (vv. 5-13). What do you think these statements mean? What do they *not* mean?**

The goal for this question is to understand that experiencing God's protection provides peace in the danger but not immunity from all harm. An honest reading of this passage will raise questions for most people. This is appropriate, and we should not shy away from seeking to understand the nature of suffering in light of what these verses promise.

These verses on the surface look like a guarantee that life will go smoothly for those who trust in God. It looks like no arrow (v. 5), disease (v. 6), violence (vv. 7-8), harm (v. 10), or poison (v. 13) will ever get through to one whose faith rests in God. Indeed, you won't even stub your toe (vv. 11-12)! In fact, these verses could be wrongly used to say that if things are going wrong in your life, it is because of a lack of faith in God.

An unbiblical interpretation of Psalm 91 is to say that God will not let faithful Christians suffer terribly, which is the way Satan wants us to read it. See the next section for more about how Satan attempts to twist these words.

The Text in the Bigger Story   (5-10 minutes)

Read Matthew 4:1-11 about the temptation of Jesus by Satan.

4. **In light of the 40 days of Lent and this season of spiritual discipline, what stood out to you as you read about Jesus' 40 days in the wilderness?**

The goal of this question is to allow the group to make associations between the season of Lent and the connection with Jesus' first days of earthly ministry. At this point in the study series, we are about halfway through Lent. Have the group consider their experiences of heightened spiritual awareness and/or physical deprivations. As the facilitator, be prepared to share from your own experiences.

5. What do you learn about the craftiness of the tempter?

It is interesting to note that Satan is familiar with the promises of the Bible and able to quote from them. We need to start with the foundational understanding that demons exist, that they believe in God and know Scripture. The Bible is clear about the reality of spiritual opponents: "For our struggle is not against flesh and blood, but against the rulers, against the authorities, against the powers of this dark world and against the spiritual forces of evil in the heavenly realms" (Ephesians 6:12).

Satan quotes Psalm 91:11 to Jesus as part of his effort to tempt him. Satan wanted Jesus to think that if the Father let him suffer, it meant his promises had failed. Jesus, however, knew that the correct interpretation of this promise is not security *from* but security *in* trouble. Verse 15 states clearly, "I will be with him *in* trouble." When we consider the entirety of Scripture, God's sure protection in and through suffering is our promise and was what Jesus experienced. Indeed, God sent ministering angels to Jesus after the temptation (v. 11).

Jesus Completing the Story   (5-10 minutes)

Have the group consider Matthew 26:36-46. Here it appears that Jesus is being tempted again, this time by his humanity and the desire to escape the brutal suffering that awaited him if he continued in obedience to the Father.

6. Consider together Matthew 26:36-46. What do we learn about the suffering of Jesus in Gethsemane? How do the promises of Psalm 91 apply to this suffering of Jesus?

Psalm 91:15 says, "He will call on me, and I will answer him; I will be with him in trouble, I will deliver him and honor him." Jesus is calling on the Father to let the cup of death pass from him. We know from the following narrative that God *did* answer his prayer, but the answer was "no." No, the cup of God's judgment would not pass from Jesus; rather, he would be obedient unto death—even the humiliating death on a cross (Philippians 2:8). This is the gospel and our hope!

Paul makes the connection for us: "What, then, shall we say in response to these things? If God is for us, who can be against us? He who did not spare his own Son, but gave him up for us all—how will he not also, along with him, graciously give us all things?" (Romans 8:31-32). God did not spare Jesus from suffering, so that we *would* be spared from eternal suffering for our sin, the punishment we rightly deserved. We are the recipients of God's most lavish promises: soul satisfaction and salvation. "With long life I will satisfy him and show him my salvation" (Psalm 91:16).

Living Out the Story   (15-20 minutes)

7. **God is speaking directly to us in verses 14-16. What does he tell us to do to experience his promises of protection? What would it look like for you to live out these practical ways of trusting God?**

In this question, guide your group to identify ways this psalm directs us to believe God's promises. In addition, you will want to push them further into what that would look like on a daily basis—in the stresses they experience and in the ways they tend to worship things other than God. All of us, in our natural bent, will work out of our own resources rather than depending on God.

Discuss ways we, as a community, can actively push each other toward Christ and away from self-reliance:

Love God (v. 14a). The word translated "love" is literally to "cleave to" or "cling to," and it is often used of human love such as the passionate love and bonding in marriage (see Genesis 34:8).

Know his name (v. 14b). To "know God's name" also means a personal relationship but one that is deeply informed by an awareness of all that he is, all his attributes and character.

Call on him (v. 15). To "call on him" means not just prayer but dependent prayer and worship.

Have the group consider past experiences of trusting God and realizing the rest and refuge he provided. Allow time for thanksgiving and praise for God's faithfulness in the midst of our suffering. Verbally expressing the goodness of God in our lives reinforces those truths above our present emotions and circumstances.

Additional Question   (to use if time allows)

The names of God listed in the first two verses (Psalm 91:1-2) describe God's character. What do you know about the meaning of these names? How could knowing these truths about God help you trust him and find refuge in him?

Allow the group a chance to talk about these names and their implications. Clarify using the definitions below:

Most High (Elyon) means "God most high," the God above all gods.

Almighty (Shaddai) indicates that God's power is sufficient in every human weakness.

The LORD (Yahweh) is the name that reveals the glory of God. It is similar to saying "I am" and communicates God's transcendence and unchanging character.

My God indicates the personal, intimate relationship possible between God and man. God is God of all, and yet he is *my* God.

The names of God evoke confidence for those who believe, as they connote the power of the Creator-Redeemer-King, as well as the endearing love of the covenantal God. The names of God remind us that there is nothing that God is or does that is not for good—both for our own ultimate good and for the good of the world. Therefore, we can trust him.

STUDY #5
Prayer for the World

Psalm 98
See page 37

The Text   (15-20 minutes)

1. Commentators call Psalm 98 a victory psalm. What kind of victory would the original readers have been thinking about when they read this psalm? How does this compare to the victory we can experience today?

Psalm 98 is a psalm that recalls in broad strokes the victories God accomplished for the Israelites. The original readers would have most likely thought of the exodus from Egypt (Exodus 15), in which God displayed supernatural power to deliver his people from bondage to Pharaoh. Readers of the psalm would also have been reminded of the battles fought by Joshua, Gideon and Samson to win the promised land of Canaan.

The saving work in this psalm is deemed marvelous, supernatural and something God has done with his "holy arm." This means that Israel's salvation from slavery was not accomplished through human effort or resources. Likewise, our salvation through Christ is accomplished by God's power and not by human effort.

God's salvation is complete and finished: "He has done marvelous things (v. 3)." The psalmist is remembering victories from the past. Our salvation through Jesus Christ is also complete. Christ's atonement for sin through his sacrifice on the cross is the final word on our sin. Our debt is paid, and we have been made right before a holy judge.

The salvation in this psalm was not done quietly, but has been made known to the whole world. Likewise, our salvation through Jesus Christ is the turning point of all history and is available to all people through faith.

2. In verse 1, the psalmist says, "Sing to the Lord a new song." Then in verses 4 through 6 he describes the praise. How does seeing the marvelous works of God prompt us to praise? What does praise do in our lives?

We naturally and spontaneously praise the things we love. We exult in the majestic wonder of a creation that is beyond understanding. We rejoice in powerful forces of rescue when we are in need of saving. Thus, when we understand the magnitude of our salvation, we can't be silent.

Consider, for example, a small parable of "being saved." Say you forgot an important deadline at work and faced damaging consequences to your credibility, and a colleague overheard your predicament and helped rescue your reputation. Your gratitude would result in praising your colleague. Imagine how much more the resulting praise for our spiritual rescue from eternal judgment!

Praising God lifts our spirits. Proverbs 17:22 says, "A cheerful heart is good medicine, but a crushed spirit dries up the bones." Focusing on what is true about God brings peace to our lives and thoughts. Philippians 2:8-9 says, "Finally, brothers and sisters, whatever is true, whatever is noble, whatever is right, whatever is pure, whatever is lovely, whatever is admirable—if anything is excellent or praiseworthy—think about such things. Whatever you have learned or received or heard from me, or seen in me—put it into practice. And the God of peace will be with you." Peace is noted here as the natural outgrowth of meditative praise.

3. How do God's saving acts "reveal his righteousness" (verse 2)? How does Jesus' death on the cross reveal his righteousness even more fully?

Theologian N. T. Wright said, "The basic meaning of 'righteousness'… denotes not so much the abstract idea of justice or virtue, as right standing and consequent right behaviour, within a community." God is righteous, and therefore his every action is just and good, both in essence and in resulting effects for his creation. This psalm makes no secret of the awesomeness of the Lord's righteousness. It is being lauded with singing and shouting (vv. 1, 4, 7).

Also revealed in this psalm is God's righteous, promise-keeping nature (v. 3). God keeps the loving and faithful promises (covenants) he made to Abraham, Moses and David. The word "love" in Hebrew means unconditional, covenant love. Despite God's insistence that the Israelites were no better than any other nation (Deuteronomy 7:7-11), he put his love on them as an act of undeserved grace and blessed the entire world through them (Genesis 12:3). Fulfilling his ancient promises,

God intervened in this world to accomplish a salvation that satisfies his righteousness—Jesus' life, death and resurrection are the ultimate realization of this psalm and the fulfillment of "the salvation he has made known to the nations" (v. 2).

The Text in the Bigger Story   (5-10 minutes)

Read Matthew 21:1-11 about Jesus' triumphal entry into Jerusalem.

4. In the psalm and in Matthew 21, we notice the resulting—and loud—worship of the glorious God who is worthy of praise because of his authority. When you consider praising God out loud, either to other Christians or to those who do not identify as Christians, what prompts your praise? What prompted the praise of the crowd in Matthew 21?

Consider first the praise of the crowd on what we call "Palm Sunday." As we know from the narrative that follows in Matthew 26 and 27, the praise of the crowd was short lived and wrongly motivated; in fact, they quickly turned on Jesus when they realized his majestic entry into Jerusalem was not heralding the kind of kingdom they wanted.

This can serve as a warning to us: Do we praise Jesus in anticipation of what he will do for us? Or do we praise him because of who he is in himself? He is "the radiance of God's glory and the exact representation of his being, sustaining all things by his powerful word" (Hebrews 1:3).

The result of one who experiences Christ's salvation is the singing of a "new song." The song is new, because the source of our wonder—the triumphant Jesus—has re-oriented our hearts to true, eternal praise. Our salvation stirs up joy in our Savior-King (Psalm 98:6). His authority is no longer threatening to us, but a matter of gladness. Further, when we acknowledge the greatness of God's deliverance, we will want to summon the whole world to praise and embrace God as their king. This was true for Israel as a light to the nations (Deuteronomy 4:5-8), and it is true for Christians today, as we are called to "let our light shine before men, that they may see your good deeds and praise your Father in heaven" (Matthew 5:14-16).

Jesus Completing the Story   (5-10 minutes)

5. In Psalm 98:7-9 all of nature joins humanity in praising God. How will God's salvation make things right, so that both mankind and all creation are free to live as God originally intended?

The goal of this question is to understand that Jesus—by his life, death, and resurrection—has begun to make all things right again in the world and will one day come again to completely renew the heaven and the earth.

During the season of Lent, we acknowledge that God's reign has begun, through the life and death of Jesus, and that God will re-establish right order and equity in the world. We are fallen people living amidst a fallen creation. Things are not the way they were meant to be. We live in the already-but-not-yet, the overlap of the beginning of Christ's kingdom and the old world of sin.

By anticipating the coming judge, we acknowledge that God's entering into his world is what will make all things right. His ultimate reign of universal peace, justice and happiness is the longing of all creation. He has already established his reign, yet all will be accomplished fully when Christ returns again. Our praise now is a prelude to the return of the great King, Jesus Christ, who will reign perfectly on earth as he does now in heaven.

We are told that when God comes back to judge the earth he will not merely put an end to evil but will also release the world from the shackles of the sin's curse (Genesis 3). Then everything on earth will be liberated to be what it was originally meant to be before sin entered into creation (Romans 8:19-21).

Living Out the Story   (15-20 minutes)

6. **Psalm 98 begins with a command to sing and ends with a picture of all creation singing together. As you journey through the season of Lent, what are some of the "marvelous things" you have experienced in your reflection on Jesus' life and death? How might you engage others in your rejoicing?**

Allow time for group members to consider their journey through Lent so far. Be prepared to share your own reflections.

Knowing that Jesus paid our penalty for sin, we experience even more "marvelous things" than the psalmist. Our sin has been paid for in Jesus! We have something to sing about. God's righteous love is both the reason Jesus had to go to the cross and the reason he did it gladly. Now the death of Jesus and his imputed righteousness make the holiness and righteousness of God not something to fear, but something to sing about.

STUDY #6
Prayer for the King

Psalm 110
See page 43

See page 43

| The Text | (15-20 minutes) |

1. The Israelites were looking forward to a messiah-king who would usher in God's reign. Describe what kind of king this psalm depicts (verses 1-3). Does Jesus fulfill these qualities? If so, how?

First, the psalm depicts the king as divine: "The LORD says to my Lord" (v. 1). The Hebrew readers believed this king would be a descendant of David, and thus would be David's "son" or descendant. Jesus, when he quotes this psalm in the gospels (Matthew 22:41-46), asserts that if David were merely foreseeing one of his descendants, he would never call him "my Lord" but rather "my son." Therefore by calling him "Lord," the text is saying that the Messiah is also divine, even God's Son.

Second, the psalm depicts the king as authoritative: "Sit at my right hand" (v. 1). Only someone with regal authority would sit at the king's right hand; therefore, the psalm depicts someone who has regal authority. It also depicts someone who has accomplished something; in this text "to sit down" conveys a finished task.

Third, the psalm indicates a presently ruling king. This king's reign begins when he is still "in the midst of your enemies" (v. 2) and will continue. The final victory, though, has not yet come. Jesus is reigning now at God's right hand (Hebrews 12:2), even though the forces of darkness continue to put forth their power.

Fourth, the psalm shows a king who is willingly followed: "Your troops will be willing on the day of your battle" (v. 3). This means that although the king has sovereign power, people want to serve and sacrifice for their king. This king has youthful vigor or an attractiveness that brings his followers into joyful, willing service (indicated by "dew of your youth" in verse 3).

In these first three verses, we have in a nutshell the person and work of Jesus, something which the entire New Testament will unpack. Jesus is divine in his person and has accomplished a great work whereby he reigns until the final consummation at the end of time.

2. **Unlike the Israelites, most modern people do not want someone else ruling their lives, as a king would necessarily do. How might Jesus as the messiah-king change your life and the lives of those around you today?**

Let your group share honestly about the implications of having a ruler like Jesus in their lives. Some aspects may cause them hesitation; others may cause rejoicing.

The Westminster Shorter Catechism states that as our king, Jesus makes us his willing subjects. He rules and defends us, while restraining and conquering all his and our enemies. As a result, we can experience:

Greater trust: The king who rules over us was also willing to die for us; thus, he can be trusted. He is not a distant, domineering king, but rather a compassionate and loving sovereign.

Greater hope: He is our defender. He is reigning now and will ultimately make all of creation right. This gives us hope and endurance: "Consider him who endured such opposition from sinful men, so that you will not grow weary and lose heart" (Hebrews 12:3).

Greater courage: His victory gives us courage. He defeated every enemy; therefore, we can face daily enemies—whether doubt and discouragement or even physical threats—with faith and perseverance. "But we are not of those who shrink back and are destroyed, but of those who believe and are saved" (Hebrews 10:39).

Greater obedience: A king commands allegiance from his followers and obedience to the laws of the kingdom. All of life should be ordered under the healing rule of Jesus.

The Text in the Bigger Story   (5-10 minutes)

Read Matthew 21:1-11 again this week, about Jesus' triumphal entry into Jerusalem, along with Zechariah 9:9.

3. Psalm 110 and Matthew 21 depict very different entries of the king. What are the most striking contrasts between the two royal entries described?

The Psalm 110 text is magisterial in its depiction; it uses commanding language:

"mighty scepter" (v. 2)
"day of battle" (v. 3)
"crush kings on the day of wrath" (v. 5)
"judge the nations, heaping up the dead" (v. 6)

In contrast, Matthew 21 depicts the Messiah as a "gentle" king. Commentators note that the prophetic words of Zechariah quoted in Matthew 21 are by no means incidental and are making the point about the nature of the new messianic administration. The Messiah would not seek to subjugate by means of military force; instead, he is called the "Prince of Peace" (Isaiah 9:6). Horses were instruments of war, while the donkey "was an appropriate mount for one who came on a mission of peace".[12]

Jesus Completing the Story   (5-10 minutes)

4. Though Jesus, the messiah-king, came in his first coming as the meek suffering servant, Psalm 110 points to his second coming in which he will have final victory over every enemy. Why can it be difficult to believe this will be true, both culturally and personally? In what ways do you need to trust him to work?

Let the group share honestly about how troubles in the world or in their lives can cause doubt in the sovereignty and power of God.

The kingdom of God was ushered in during the ministry and death of Jesus, but it is not yet fully realized. Because powers of evil are still present, it is easy to focus on what is not made right, rather than what is and what will be. Like the temporarily adoring crowds on Palm Sunday, we can be spiritually myopic, expecting that Jesus will reign in ways we anticipate or answer prayers in ways we prefer. How quickly we forget that he is the Christ, the Son of God; he is the Christ, and we are not!

As the true King, he will ultimately subjugate the enemies of the whole human race—sin, death, and evil. Psalm 110 doesn't hide the fact that his judgment will be earth shattering and bloody. We hold in tension the

---

[12] J.G. Baldwin, *Haggai, Zechariah, Malachi — Tyndale Old Testament Commentaries* (Downers Grove, Ill: Intervarsity Press, 1972), 166.

teaching of these texts, that the conquering King Jesus of Psalm 110 is also the Prince of Peace, "gentle and riding on a donkey" (Zechariah 9:9).

Living Out the Story   (15-20 minutes)

5. What difference would it make in your life if you regularly experienced Jesus as your priest and king?

Jonathan Edwards writes, "The lion excels in strength and in the majesty of his appearance and voice. The lamb excels in meekness and patience, and is sacrificed for food and clothing. There is in Jesus, a conjunction of such really diverse excellencies as otherwise would have seemed to us utterly incompatible in the same subject."[13] He is both majestic and meek, all glorious and all loving. We cannot fully comprehend his excellencies, but we can trust him. This assurance is where we base our identity.

Additionally, we his followers are called to be kings and priests also, not serving ourselves but serving within God's kingdom and declaring his praises (1 Peter 2:9). Allow the group to consider the specific ways their lives would be different—perhaps in service, vocation, leisure time, relationships—if they lived out their calling of being a "royal priesthood, a people belonging to God" (1 Peter 2:9-21 could be a helpful place to point the group).

6. Looking back on this study, what do you need to repent of in order to follow Jesus, our powerful king and priest? How can the group pray for you about this?

Allow the group to share honestly about their struggles and unbelief. As the facilitator, be prepared to share your own areas of unbelief. Perhaps reflect on the past six weeks of Lent and the ways in which you and your group members have drawn nearer to God and one another.

Close the study by reading a scripture selection from either Zechariah 9 (the prophecy of Jesus entering Jerusalem) or 1 Peter 2 (instructions for Christian believers).

---

[13] Jonathan Edwards in his sermon "The Admirable Conjunction of Diverse Excellencies in Christ Jesus."

STUDY #7
Prayer for Security

Psalm 16
See page 49

The Text **(15-20 minutes)**

1. In the opening line, David cries out to God, asking to be kept safe. According to the text, what is threatening David? How does your need for safety parallel that of David?

Though there are many evils in the world that can be a threat, there are two main pressures David is experiencing in Psalm 16.[14] First is the scorn of those who don't share his beliefs. David feels threatened by the mocking and the pressure of those who "run after other gods" (v. 4). David's beliefs and spiritual commitments are being called into question by those around him who don't share those beliefs, and David feels attacked and in need of refuge. In its broadest sense, then, this pressure David is feeling is the pressure to "fit in," when fitting in would mean dishonoring his commitment to God.

Secondly, David is experiencing the threat of his own mortality. Though he does not appear to be in imminent danger, David senses the unavoidable, that death looms in the distance (vv. 9-10). The word "grave" in verse 10 is, in older versions of the Bible, translated *sheol*, the "place of the dead." In the biblical tradition this is a place of darkness and great discomfort (cf. Luke 16:19-31). So, in this psalm David is looking to God to keep him safe from present attacks and to provide some kind of life beyond the grave.

---

[14] John Goldingay, *Psalms, Vol. 1: Psalms 1-41* (Baker Commentary on the Old Testament Wisdom and Psalms), (Grand Rapids, Mich: Baker Academic, 2006), 228.

2. According to Psalm 16:5, what words does David use to describe God? What do you think those images suggest?

Employing metaphorical language, David calls God his "portion" and his "cup":

1. David calls God his "portion," meaning his security and stability. The word *portion* in the Old Testament is often used to designate the plot of land that belonged to someone, whether that land was purchased or given as an inheritance. Someone's portion of land was crucial for his livelihood, as it was his home, his source of security from harsh elements and enemies, and his source of income in an agrarian society.

2. David calls God his "cup," meaning his condition of life. Throughout the Old Testament the word *cup* functions as a metaphor for an individual's fate, and here David expresses gratitude for God's allowance of security, peace and "pleasant places."

By putting these two rich images together, David shows that God is the one who has given him security, stability, joy, love, peace and meaning. David realizes that the Lord is his portion. No matter what is going on around him, David knows that God is what his heart most needs and desires.

3. According to Psalm 16:6-7, what has God done for David? In what ways would knowing God like this influence the way you see your life?

First, God has given David a beautiful inheritance. Building on the "portion" imagery from verse 5, David points out that God has made the "boundary lines fall in pleasant places." In David's day one plot of land was delineated and allocated from another portion of land by setting up markers to distinguish the boundaries of one person's property from another.[15] Of course, some plots of lands were more desirable than others (for their fertility, location, etc.). David is speaking metaphorically here, but what he is communicating is that God has marked out his plot (his life), and it is a beautiful inheritance.

For God's people today, their beautiful inheritance includes peace with God, the promise of his presence, the knowledge that he works all things together for their ultimate good, and the hope of a bright and glorious future in his presence.

Second, God has provided David with daily guidance as he navigates his way through life. God is the one who counsels David, and the basic meaning of the word "counsel" is advice about how one ought to live.

---

[15] Goldingay, *Psalms*, 231.

The primary way God provides this guidance for his people today is through the instruction of his Word. In addition, oftentimes God uses others in community to help us better understand his Word as we seek to be guided through it. As one author notes, "The Psalmist praises God because of the experience of having been guided through life by God's good and gracious law. Without this counsel, the Psalmist might have wandered blindly down the path to destruction."[16]

The Text in the Bigger Story   (5-10 minutes)

Read together Acts 2:22-33.

4. **In Acts 2 the apostle Peter interprets Psalm 16 to be looking forward to Jesus' resurrection. Why is it important that Peter quotes this particular psalm?**

By quoting from Psalm 16, Peter is emphatically pointing out that the resurrection of Christ was a physical, bodily resurrection. Just like today, there were people in the first-century Jerusalem who denied the literal, bodily resurrection of Jesus Christ. The British theologian N.T. Wright points out, "The whole passage [Acts 2] only makes the sense it was intended to make if the resurrection is thought of as a bodily event in which Jesus' physical body did not decay as those of the patriarchs had done, but received new life."[17]

Furthermore, by quoting this psalm, a psalm of David, Peter is saying that the Lord Jesus is distinct from every other Old Testament hero, because while David died, only the Lord Jesus defeated death and rose again bodily. Since Christ alone has burst the bonds of death by virtue of his resurrection, he alone is the Messiah whom David foresaw.

Jesus Completing the Story   (5-10 minutes)

5. **What can we learn about Peter using this text in his first recorded sermon? What does this tell us about how the early Christians read Scripture?**

Peter is speaking to a group of his peers, fellow Hebrews who questioned the claim of Jesus as the promised Messiah. Although he himself had come to acknowledge Jesus as Messiah earlier (see Luke 9:20), Peter knows the doubts his fellow countrymen have. He does not

---

16 Nancy L. deClaissé-Walford, *The Book of Psalms*, The New International Commentary on the Old Testament (Cambridge: Eerdmans, 2014), 181.
17 N. T. Wright, *The Resurrection of the Son of God* (Minneapolis: Fortress, 2003), 455.

appeal just to the signs and wonders displayed by Jesus (Acts 2:22), he goes for the most powerful explanation he has at his disposal—the holy Scriptures. In a world before printing presses, oral histories and Torah recitations were the vehicles for education. Peter's use of Psalm 16, a scripture everyone knew, was the most logical case he could make in his argument for the bodily resurrection of Jesus.

That Peter quotes this passage tells us something about how he and other early Christians read Scripture. The earliest Christians saw everything in Scripture—absolutely everything—as pointing to Jesus. The Bible, then, is primarily about what God has done in Christ, not merely a book about what we are supposed to do for God.

What all this means, then, is that the Lord is able to deliver his people from all their fears, for he has already defeated the greatest of all enemies, death itself. God is faithful, not only in this life, but in a life beyond the grave.

Living Out the Story   (5-10 minutes)

6. In his book *Miracles*, C.S. Lewis wrote about Jesus' resurrection saying, "[Jesus] has met, fought, and beaten the King of Death. Everything is different because he has done so."[18] If it's true that Jesus was raised from the dead, how should your life be different? How is the whole world different?

This question provides occasion to reflect on the practical implications of Easter. If Christ really defeated death, how are our lives as individuals and as members of this community affected? As your group members share, invite them to be as practical and as personal as they can.

Consider for example:

How does Christ's resurrection affect the ways we think about evil and suffering in the world?
The resurrection means that one day all evil will be defeated and God's justice and glory will cover the earth "as the waters cover the sea" (Isaiah 11:9). We can work for justice now in light of that hope.

How does Christ's resurrection affect the ways we think about our own mortality?
Like David, we are often consumed with our own mortality and fear about the future. Easter means, however, the defeat of death and freedom from fear of death. God's power, "which he exerted

---

[18] C.S. Lewis, *Miracles* (New York: Harper, 2000), 237.

in Christ when he raised him from the dead,"[19] is a reality for us, both in life and death. In a world riddled with violence, disease and grief, this hope can bring a sturdy, settling peace that "transcends all understanding" (Philippians 4:6-7).

---

[19] Ephesians 1:19-21.

How does God's generosity make us generous?

Generosity: Responding to God's Radical Grace in Community
A Seven-Session Study Guide by Redeemer Presbyterian Church
ISBN-13: 978-1-944549-00-8

Generosity: How God's Radical Grace Changes Our Perspective on Money and Possessions
A 20-Day Devotional Booklet by Andrew Field &
Redeemer Presbyterian Church
ISBN-13: 978-1-944549-01-5

Generosity: How God's Radical Grace Makes Us Givers
A Seven-Part Sermon Series from Timothy Keller & Abraham Cho
DVD set ISBN-13: 978-1-944549-02-2

For more information on the Generosity series and other items related to generosity, visit **gospelinlife.com/generosity**

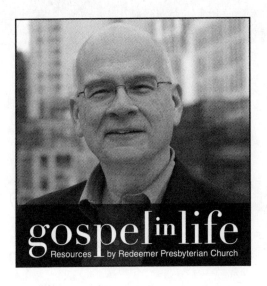

We invite you to visit gospelinlife.com where you can browse over 25 years of sermons and resources by Timothy Keller and the staff of Redeemer Presbyterian Church.

View the 10 most popular sermon series:
gospelinlife.com/top10

This list includes a nine-part series on marriage from Ephesians 5, which was the basis for the best-selling book *The Meaning of Marriage*.